Breaking the
Chains of Bondage

Dr. (Rev.) Paul E. Scull, DC/Psy

"Catch us the foxes, the little foxes
that spoil the vines, for our vines
have tender grapes."
Song of Solomon 2:15 (NKJV)

Acknowledgements

I would like to thank Chris Hickman for the typing and retyping portions of this book to help formulate its final form. Cassandra Rodriguez for the artwork on the cover of the book. Barb Bybel for writing the chapter on Inner Healing.

My wife for reading the manuscript and input on the use of wording throughout the text. Donna Lane for the final proofreading of this book.

A thank you to Joan Hunter and Righteous Acts Ministries for the use of their material.

Table of Contents

Part I
How Does Satan Trap Us?

Part II
Knowing Your History and Taking Care of It

Appendix

Introduction

As the last days are approaching, God is giving us more and more revelation on how to set ourselves and others free. New insights and revelation on how to pray for the sick, the breaking of demonic strongholds, inner healing, the erasing of bad memories to help those with PTSD and those struggling with pornography, the breaking of blood covenants, and the spiritual side of addictions that keep people in bondage, are all insights God is showing us in these last days to set us free.

Hosea 4:6 (HCSB) states, "My people are destroyed for lack of knowledge. Because you have rejected knowledge, I will reject you from serving as My priest. Since you have forgotten the law of your God, I will also forget your sons."

God is giving us this knowledge, so our people (you and me) will not perish but will be able to put on the full armor of God to withstand these end times.

We need to be free, so we can go and set others free also. "Therefore if the Son sets you free, you really will be free." John 8:36 (HCSB)

Dr. (Rev.) Paul E. Scull

Authority of the Believer

First Level of Authority

"Summoning His 12 disciples, He gave them authority over unclean spirits, to drive them out and to heal every disease and sickness...." Jesus sent out these 12 after giving them instructions: "Don't take the road leading to other nations and don't enter any Samaritan town. Instead, go to the lost sheep of the house of Israel." Matthew 10: 1, 5-6 (HCSB)

The 12 Disciples – gave **authority over** unclean spirits, **healed every** disease and sickness; went only to the **house** of Israel.

Second Level of Authority

"After this, the Lord appointed 70 others, and He sent them ahead of Him in pairs to every town and place...Heal the sick who are there and tell them, The kingdom of God has come near you ... Look, I have given you the authority to trample on snakes and scorpions, and over all the power of the enemy, nothing will ever harm you." Luke 10:1, 9, 19 (HCSB)

The 70 - gave **authority to trample** on snakes and scorpions, **over all** the **power** of the enemy **nothing would harm** them; went into **every town** and **place**.

Third Level of Authority

"Go into all the world and preach the gospel to the whole creation. Whoever believes and is baptized will be saved, but whoever does not believe will be condemned. And these signs will accompany those who believe: In My Name, they will drive out demons; they will speak in new languages; they will pick up snakes; if they should drink anything deadly, it will never harm them; they will lay hands on the sick, and they will get well." Mark 16:15-18 (HCSB)

Us the believers – Go to **every nation**. You shall **take up serpents,** and if you **drink** any **deadly poison,** it will not hurt you.

Protection both inside and out!

Part I

How Does Satan Trap Us?

Those Besetting Sins

I have been involved with healing and our counseling ministry for 29 years and yet, after counseling and praying for healing, many people were still not healed or still did not have the victory in those areas of their life in which "the sin which doth so easily beset us...." Hebrews 12:1 (KJV)

I even struggled with issues from being sexually abused at age five and struggled with sexual addiction later on in life.

I went for counseling and healing and, even though I was healed of all outward signs and the acting out of the sins from the effect of the sexual abuse and addiction, the videos of the abuse and pornography pictures continued to play over and over in my mind.

The emotional toll of fighting these videos day in and day out became draining, and I was still not, in my opinion, entirely set free as Jesus stated in John 8:38.

The Lord led me to two ministries which have changed my life. About seven years ago, I went to Righteous Acts Ministries for deliverance and training in the program of Rev. Bill Sudduth. This helped tremendously. I came back and added this remarkable deliverance ministry to our healing and counseling programs. Once I added this deliverance ministry to our ministry, we had a year's waiting list for individuals who wanted to be set free.

About two years ago, I went to a Joan Hunter Conference. While there, Joan said she was going to pray, and God was going to erase the memory of the past. I leaned over and told my wife at that time "That's stupid, no one can erase your memories."

Boy, was I wrong! After Joan's prayer, I still knew I was sexually abused, but all the memories and those videos that were continually playing in my head were gone. I used to remember all the sexual abuse acts, all the pornography pictures, and even an X-rated movie that was shown to me when I was seven years old. After that prayer, I could not bring up or recall any of it – praise God!

My wife, having lived with me for 40-plus years, was a little skeptical – I didn't blame her. She keeps asking me, at first about every five minutes, "How about now," are they gone?" Over time, the "how about now" grew less often and she now also believes that I am totally set free.

But I was wondering if it would work on others. A friend of mine, who was a Vietnam War veteran who had a hard time going to sleep at night because of the pictures and images and sounds of war which would keep him awake, came to me for prayer. I prayed the simple trauma prayer, asking God to erase the memories of the war. The next Sunday he came to me and told me his mind was completely free from those pictures, images, and sounds of war. He went right to sleep and slept all night. He is still free to this day!

So, we go through our Christian life working out our salvation: praying, going to church, reading the Bible, and fasting. Many of us still struggle with "those sins that so easily beset us." Why?

The word salvation can be translated "SOZO." In the Greek, it means salvation (eternal life), healing, and deliverance. We have our salvation down but don't understand or are not taught that we should be working out our healing and deliverance, just like our salvation, "with trembling and fear."

Since we don't, we go through life defeated, poor, and sick with addictions, low self-esteem, unforgiveness, strongholds, and other struggles.

This is not what God wants for us. Being free in Christ is being free in body, soul, and mind – salvation, healing, and deliverance.

This book will help you get rid of those "sins that so easily beset us." As long as we struggle with sickness, unforgiveness, strongholds, and defeat, Satan has us right where he wants us, and we are no threat to his kingdom.

Isn't it time you took your life back and let your light shine for all to see?

Why Do We Struggle?

Why do Christians struggle with life issues, family and marriage problems, poverty, long-term illness, sickness, so on and so forth, over and over? Even the Apostle Paul himself said, "For what I am doing, I do not understand. For what I will to do, that I do not practice; but what I hate, that I do." Romans 7:15 (NKJV)

Why does it seem that Christians have to struggle for months and years before they get the victory in an area of their life? Some Christians never seem to get the victory no matter how hard they try. I had struggled with the effects of sexual abuse and sexual addiction for over 20 years. I would pray, read my Bible, go to church, whatever I could – yet I still struggled with the effects of the abuse and still had no lasting effect or healing.

I don't think it is God who wants us to fight for years and years with these sins. Not until the last seven years did I learn to get free and also how to set others free, and not only set ourselves free but to stay free!

"Dear friend, I pray that you may prosper in every way and be in good health, just as your soul prospers." 3 John 2 (HCSB). Our soul includes our mind, will, and emotions. When we are saved, the same spirit that lives in Christ lives in us. Our spirit becomes Christ-like, but getting saved does not instantly perfect our soul (mind, will, and emotions). But we are being "conformed to the image of Christ" (Romans 8:29). Because our soul is still in the process of becoming Christlike, the events, such as divorce, accidents, and other trauma, can leave scars or wounds in our inner man (soul). If we do not deal with these events or traumas, they can cause all kinds of sickness and behavior problems.

When we sin, or someone sins against us, this can also cause a trauma or a wound. These types of trauma could be abuse, adultery, pornography, and all kinds of addiction.

The sins and traumas in your life create wounds that give Satan legal access rights to afflict, depress, harass, and cause sickness and behavioral problems in your soul.

7

Satan comes to kill, steal and destroy. If he cannot do it outright, he tries to ruin our Christian witness. Since Satan is not omnipresent like God, he cannot be everywhere at the same time, so he sends his demons. Demons are fallen angels that fell with Satan when he was kicked out of heaven when he tried to usurp God's power.

Demons can be both large and small and aggressive or can come as an angel of light. They constantly do Satan's bidding. This book is not meant to deal in depth with Satan and the demonic.[1] Appendix B goes into some detail on sexual demons.

We know Christians cannot be demon-possessed. But Christians can be oppressed, depressed, and have strongholds in their lives.

These strongholds also give Satan access rights to us through generational curses, witchcraft, unforgiveness, covenants, and other such doors that we opened or were opened by others. The sins, traumas, affliction, depression,

---

[1] See Appendix B "*What About the Demonic?*"

harassment, sickness and behavioral problems in your soul can create wounds that give Satan legal access right to us also.

"And the very God of peace sanctify you wholly, and I pray God your whole spirit and soul and body be preserved blameless unto the coming of our Lord Jesus Christ. 1 Thessalonians 5:23 (KJV) Our spirt is the Spirit realms our body is our flesh, and our soul consist of our mind, will, and emotions.

The **spirit** – it's our spirit that gets saved - is the place where the Holy Spirit dwells. Once saved, Satan cannot possess or touch our spirit it belongs to God.

The **soul** – "Beloved I wish above all things that thou mayest prosper and be in health, even as thy soul prospereth." III John 2 (KJV)

Notice it says "soul;" it's not how spiritual we are but how healthy our soul is. When Christians go through trials, the first thing they do is get more spiritual when in fact they should be working on getting their soul healthy.

What we think and say about the abuse and trauma of life all affects our soul. The soul is our emotions, thoughts, feelings and will. "And be not conformed to this world: but be ye transformed by the renewing of your mind, that ye may prove what is that good, and acceptable, and perfect, will of God." Romans 12:2 (KJV). Our mind must be renewed to speak life not death to our situations.

The **body** – in turn, our soul with all its damage affects our body. These issues that we have not dealt with can come out in the form of illness and sickness, and some of these issues build strongholds from the enemy.

1 Thessolonians 5:23

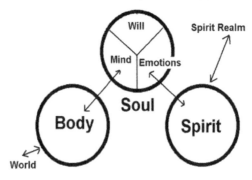

The sins and traumas in your life create wounds that give Satan legal access right to afflict, depress, harass, and cause sickness and behavioral problems in your soul.

It is up to us to close those doors to Satan.

What Are Strongholds?

A stronghold in our life is any area, which we do not have control over or cannot get the victory over in a particular area in our life.

Once these strongholds are formed, Satan has access to control our emotions, thoughts, and our sin patterns.

This is why we continue to struggle with those "sins that so easily beset us." We can't break those addictions, continuing lust, struggle with pornography, anger, jealousy, low self-esteem, abuse issues, trauma, etc. because we have not dealt with the root of these issues and Satan has access rights to these areas and thoughts that control our lives.

Satan will not give up those access rights with just a simple prayer. You must close those doors that gave Satan those access rights to you.

Part II

Knowing Your History and Taking Care of It

Imprints

Satan keeps the images, memories, and emotions alive in our head through imprints.

Our mind is made so that every experience that we have, good or bad, from birth to death, releases a chemical that imprint, that event on our mind. These imprints can be from our five senses or any real trauma that we go through.

We, humans, form regular behavior patterns as we grow, learning proper behavior. But when a child is abused, physically, emotionally, or sexually, or in some other way traumatized it causes him or her to develop a behavior pattern that is not normal and, if not corrected, the child will struggle with that pattern for the rest of his or her life.

Science says we have as many filing cabinets to store our memories and trauma in our mind as there are stars in the universe. Much like we can't number the stars, the filing cabinets in our mind that store these events, good or bad, are unlimited.

If we do not deal with the bad events (memories/traumas), they cause us to develop bad habits or sin, and Satan uses them to plague us for the rest of our lives.

Satan does not play fair. He uses every trick in his book to deceive us. Remember, it's the little foxes that spoil the vine.

Setting Ourselves Free Unforgiveness

Unforgiveness is one of the major obstacles to healing and deliverance.

We had someone who came to us for deliverance. When it came time for this individual to forgive certain people in their life, they said they couldn't. At that point, we stopped the deliverance process.

God will not go against His Word. He will not hear, heal or deliver you unless you forgive others. "And whenever you stand praying, if you have anything against anyone, forgive him, so that your Father in heaven will also forgive you your wrongdoing." Mark 11:25 (HCSB)

Forgiveness is not something we always feel. We go through the forgiveness prayer and believe God has set us free. The battle is won in the renewing of our minds. We must learn to switch our negative thinking to positive things. "Finally, brethren, whatsoever things are true, whatsoever things are honest, whatsoever things are just, whatsoever things are pure, whatsoever things are lovely, whatsoever things are of good report; if there be any virtue, and if there be any praise, think on these things." Philippines 4:8 (KJV)

For years, our minds have been like a railroad track. Our negative thoughts keep traveling down them on a straight line. But now every time a negative thought comes, we need to switch that negative thought to a positive one. Every negative thought must be canceled and our new thoughts rerouted on the new track. We need to rewire our brain to think only positive thoughts.

I used to be the sickest person on staff. One day I asked my pastor if I could start a Healing Room ministry. He laughed at me, knowing I was the sickest person he had on staff.

I knew my faith for healing was low and that I had to switch my negative tracks to positive ones, so I picked up a confession book about healing.[2] To renew my mind about healing, I started reading those confessions three times a

---

[2] Charles Capp, "*God's Creative Power for Healing.*"

day for seven months. That is how much I had to renew my mind on healing before I could believe for myself and others.

Once my mind was renewed, then I started our Healing Rooms.

We need to do this with forgiveness. Every time something negative comes to our mind about a person that we have forgiven, we must switch our track in our mind to positive thoughts. Keep at it until you make that new track and finally it will become automatic.

Forgiveness

Unforgiveness is one of the major obstacles to healing. Please take the time to list any and all individuals, including yourself and God, if needed, that you need to forgive.

In your list include anyone who has hurt you emotionally, physically, verbally, or spiritually.

Note: If you were sexually abused, please list your perpetrators in your forgiveness prayer.

Prayer for Forgiveness

Lord, your Word tells us "to prosper and be in health even as our soul prospers." By not forgiving you, myself or others, I have given Satan legal grounds to build strongholds of unforgiveness in my life.

I renounce self-condemnation and self-judgment, and receive your forgiveness and ask you to cleanse my heart.

I choose right now to forgive my offenders. (name them if need be) I release them all into your hands. I give up every "right" to harbor any resentment. I turn them all completely over to you.

Bring my emotions into alignment with my choice for forgiveness. Guide me as I strive to build a stronghold of compassion. Please guard my heart so that no root of bitterness can spring up again.

I now set myself free from all spirits and strongholds of unforgiveness in Jesus' Name! Amen.

Generational Curses

Generational curses can provide Satan with access rights to our mind, body, and emotions. Some believe that Christians can't have curses. If you don't like the word "curses," you can use the words "DNA" or "ancestral traits."

All I know is that both good and bad hereditary traits come down the family line. My father was left-handed, I am left-handed, and my daughter is left-handed. Being left-handed is a good thing. Judges 20:16 (NKJV) tells us, "Among all this people were seven hundred select men who were left-handed; every one could sling a stone at a hair's breadth and not miss." What accuracy! What eyesight! I receive it in Jesus' Name! I also know that my grandmother had a child out of wedlock, my father had girlfriends, and I turned to sexual addiction as my drug of choice.

So you can see that both good and bad traits can come down through your ancestral line.

God also tell us "You must not bow down to them or worship them; for I, the Lord your God, am a jealous God, punishing the children for the fathers' sin, to the third and fourth generations, of those who hate Me ..." Exodus 20:5 (HCSB), and again He states "No one of illegitimate birth may enter the Lord's assembly; none of his descendants, even to the tenth generation, may enter the Lord's Assembly." Deuteronomy 23:2 (HCSB)

But there is good news. God will forgive our ancestors' sins if we ask Him to and He will break the curses. "But if they will confess their sin and the sin of their fathers – their unfaithfulness that they practiced against Me, and how they acted with hostility toward Me, ... and if their uncircumcised hearts will be humbled, and if they will pay the penalty for their sin, then I will remember My covenant with Jacob, I will also remember my covenant with Isaac and my covenant with Abraham, and I will remember the land." Leviticus 26:40-42 (NKJV).

To close the generational curses in your ancestral line, you will need to go through the following prayer. If there is a particular curse you need to break such as cancer, diabetes, anger, or sexual issues, add it as you pray for yourself.

Prayer to Break Generational Curses

Father, I now ask that you forgive my forefathers for their sins back unto the fifth generation.

If there was anyone in my forefather's line who had a child or children out of wedlock, I ask that this specific sin is also forgiven back unto the tenth generation and the curses stated in Deuteronomy 28:59 of severe and lasting plagues and terrible and chronic sickness be broken in Jesus' Name.

Now, in the Name of Jesus Christ and by the power of His blood, I renounce, break, and sever all forms of curses, iniquities and generational curses that have come down through my ancestral lines. I set myself free in Jesus' Name! Amen.

Soul Ties

A soul tie is the knitting of two souls that can either bring tremendous blessings in a Godly relationship or great destruction when made with the wrong person. An example of a soul tie is that of Jonathan and David. "And it came to pass when he had made an end of speaking unto Saul that the soul of Jonathan was knitted with the soul of David, and Jonathan loved him as his own soul." 1 Samuel 18:1 (KJV) The Hebrew word for "knit" means "wrapped around one another." Thus, we could say "... Jonathan's soul was wrapped around the soul of David ...."

The stronger the soul tie or bonding, the deeper and more lasting the relationship. A person can control another through soul ties because of the mind, will, and emotions of the two individuals are now open to one another. In ungodly relationships, these soul ties may place us in emotional and mental bondage to others.

In marriage, Genesis 2:24 (NKJV) tells us, "Therefore shall a man leave his father and his mother, and shall cleave unto his wife; and they shall be one flesh," meaning their souls are wrapped around each other.

If the ungodly soul ties to their parents are not broken, when the two people are married, the conflict will eventually arise. Have you ever hear of a "Mamma's Boy"?

Genesis 2:23 (NKJV) states "... this is now bone of my bone and flesh of my flesh ..." and in Ephesians 5:30-31 (KJV) "we become one with the Lord."

The soul tie formed through the sexual union of marriage is real. Since the sexual union of marriage ties two souls as one, what do you think happens if a person commits fornication or adultery, or has sex with another individual prior or during the marriage?

Your soul becomes knitted or tied to those other individuals through those illicit sexual acts. These sexual involvements can be as strong and binding as those formed through the marriage covenant.

Genesis 34: 1-3 (KJV) gives us an example of an ungodly soul tie: "And Dinah the daughter of Leah, which she bare unto Jacob, went out to see the daughters of the land. And, when Shechem, the son of Hamor the Hivite, prince of the country, saw her, he took her, lay with her, and defiled her. And, his soul clave unto Dinah, the daughter of Jacob, and he loved the damsel and spake kindly unto the damsel."

The consequences of a casual affair can be harmful and enduring. The soul ties formed can bind a person for life. For instance, God has so built every woman that the first man who has sexual relations with her "takes dominion over her." (Genesis 3:16) Her human spirit and soul are built to respond to that man by nurturing him, supplying affection to him, and being that man's fountain of satisfaction and blessing all through his life.

This kind of soul tie gives a man dominion over his wife or lover and is often so binding that he can insult and mistreat her, but she seems helplessly enslaved to him. She can be verbally, physically, or sexually abused, and yet she is unable and often unwilling to leave. Often, even if she does manage to leave such a man, she finds herself compelled to return to him. What do you think happens to people who have formed soul ties with many people through fornication and promiscuity?

In reality, their souls have become fragmented and scattered among all their sexual partners. They are unable to give themselves entirely to their spouse. Their thoughts and emotions are continually drawn back to their past lovers.

At this point, if you have had any wrong sexual imprints or ungodly sexual soul ties, you need to go through the following prayer. This prayer will break the emotional and sexual desires (ungodly soul ties) you are having or had with these individuals.

You need to make a list of individuals that you have had sexual contact with before or during marriage.

Note: An ungodly soul tie can be formed through sex with anyone outside of marriage, with fantasy partners, by the pornography you watched, masturbation, lust or the reading or looking at any sexual books or novels. You will also need to break any ungodly soul ties with individuals you have become two emotionally attached to parents, children, or another individual.

You need to go through the following prayer that breaks these ungodly sexual covenants and soul ties. It might be a good idea to have someone with you, a trusted friend, counselor or your pastor as you verbalize this prayer.

Prayer to Break Ungodly Sexual Soul Ties

Heavenly Father, I submit myself wholly to you. I ask you to forgive me for any and all unnatural or ungodly relationships with any person, place or thing. I ask you to forgive me for any, and all sexual misconduct or ungodly soul ties, specifically with (make a list if you need to) and name the individuals. (naming the individual can be done out loud or under your breath if someone else is leading you through this prayer.)

And in the mighty Name of Jesus, I ask that my spirit be loosed from them according to Matthew 18:18-19 and I tell my spirit to forget the unions. I tell my mind to release responsibility for them, and I tell my emotions to let go and forget the unions. I tell the fragmented pieces of my soul to come back together. I hereby break every ungodly soul tie in the mighty Name of Jesus.

Lord, I choose to forgive each person that I have been involved with in any wrong way. I renounce all uses of my body as an instrument of unrighteousness, and by so doing, I ask you to break all bondages that Satan has brought into my life through that involvement.

I confess my participation, I choose to forgive myself, and I choose to be no longer angry with myself or to hate myself or punish myself. I now present my body to you as a living sacrifice, holy and acceptable to you. I reserve the sexual use of my body only for marriage. I renounce the lie of Satan that my body is not clean, that it is dirty or in any way unacceptable as a result of my past sexual experience.

Lord, I thank you that you have totally cleansed and forgiven me and that you love and accept me unconditionally. Therefore, I can accept myself, and I choose to accept myself, and my body is cleansed, In Jesus' Name. Amen!"[3]

---

[3] Acknowledgment for the "Soul Ties Prayer" is given to Teresa Castleman's book "Brownville Deliverance Manual" 1996-97.

Blood Covenants

Trauma that happens to an individual stays in that person's body. When you receive transfusions, transplants, insulin or vaccinations, you are receiving the blood from someone else. Their blood can carry the trauma through the generational curses and can be transferred to you.

In John 20:23 (NKJV) it says, "If you forgive the sins of any, they are forgiven them; if you retain the sins of any, they are retained." This is why these prayers are needed.

Children and adults may make blood covenants by pricking their fingers or cutting themselves and exchanging blood, becoming "blood brothers" with other individuals. Doors to generational curses can be opened through something as simple as pricking your finger or cutting yourself and mixing or smearing your blood with someone else. These covenants need to be broken.

Perhaps the other person is living for the devil, and you do not understand why living for Jesus has been so stressful for you. Your covenant partner's actions do and can affect you through his bloodline.

Prayer to Break the Pricking of the Finger

In Jesus' Name, I renounce the covenant I made with (person's name) with the cutting or pricking of our fingers and the mixing of our blood with my friends to make a blood pack with them.

I break that blood covenant off of me now through the blood line of their ancestors and renounce all generational curses from their blood line with the mixing of our blood. I renounce that blood pack that was made with (person's name) at that time.

I set myself free in Jesus' Name. Amen.

Blood Transfusions, Transplants, Insulin or Vaccinations

(Here again, you are breaking the generational curses from the individual's bloodline.)

By receiving an organ or a blood transfusion from another person, there could be the transference of generational curses from the blood transfer.

Prayer for Blood Transfusions and Transplants

I repent for the sins of the person or persons whose (body part, blood transfusions) I have received.

Any transference of generational curses that came in through (body parts, blood transfusion) are cut off from me now in Jesus' Name! Amen.

Ungodly Covenants

Some covenants are the result of sexual abuse, rape or molestation. You need to break these unwanted and ungodly covenants and ungodly soul ties and forgive the person(s) who assaulted you.

Prayer to Break Ungodly Covenants from Sexual Abuse, Rape or Molestation

Father, the ungodly covenant that was forced upon me from (name person or persons), I now dissolve. I also dissolve any ungodly soul ties with that/those individuals in Jesus' Name.

I renounce and break that ungodly covenant and soul tie now in Jesus' Name. I close all doors or access rights now that Satan had in my life because of that or those covenants or ungodly soul ties.

I now forgive each individual from that or those ungodly convents and set myself totally free from all the physical and emotional pain in Jesus' Name. I release all shame and guilt and ask you to erase all the negative memories from these ungodly covenants.

I thank you for setting me free in the Name of Jesus. Amen!

Divorce

In the early Church, the highest gift a man could receive from God was a wife. "Whoso findeth a wife findeth a good thing and obtaineth favor of the Lord." Proverbs: 18:22 (KJV) It is interesting to note there is no word for "bachelor" in the Hebrew language.

This covenant was a physical consummation of the marriage. Marriage covenants are meant to be permanent, and sin is always to blame when a marriage ends in divorce. This statement is not intended to blame anyone. We know there are circumstances in which marriages are broken up.

This book does not have the space to go into detail on the subject of marriage and divorce.

Marriage is a covenant. Covenants themselves are very powerful and binding. A marriage covenant vows both parties unto death.

Once divorced, it is important for you to break not only soul ties with your ex-spouse but also break that covenant of death you made with them.

Prayer for Breaking Covenant of Divorce

Father, I made a marriage covenant with my (name your ex-spouse).

Now that I am no longer married to him/her, that covenant is no longer valid. The covenant of "unto death do us part" is now void and broken in Jesus' Name. I ask you to remove anything ungodly that came in through that covenant and remove it from me now in Jesus' Name! Amen.

Witchcraft, Occult, and Transference of Spirits

Astrology, Horoscope, Occult and New Age all help Satan to trap us in his web of deception.

It's not the Ouija board, the prophecy of the horoscope, or the astrology symbols that are the problems per se. It is what's behind the meaning of these symbols and the demonic influence and covenants that are made with Satan when you dabble in them.

It's the same thing with Freemasonry, lodges, fraternities, and sororities. It's what's behind them in the spiritual realm that transfers to us, not the outward appearance of their good deeds.[4]

---

[4] For a thorough understanding of the evil of Freemasonry see the DVD by Bill Sudduth *"Freemasonry"*.

Transference of Spirits

Numbers 13:23-33 (HCSB) is a good example of this. "When they came to the Valley of Eshcol, they cut down a branch with a single cluster of grapes, which was carried on a pole by two men. They also took some pomegranates and figs. That place was called the Valley of Eshcol because of the cluster of grapes the Israelites cut there. At the end of 40 days, they returned from scouting out the land. The men went back to Moses, Aaron, and the entire Israelite community in the Wilderness of Paran at Kadesh. They brought back a report for them and the whole community, and they showed them the fruit of the land. They reported to Moses: 'We went into the land where you sent us. Indeed it is flowing with milk and honey, and here is some of its fruit. However, the people living in the land are strong, and the cities are large and fortified. We also saw the descendants of Anak there. The Amalekites are living in the land of the Negev; the Hittites, Jebusites, and Amorites live in the hill country; and the Canaanites live by the sea and along the Jordan.' Then Caleb quieted the people in the presence of Moses and said, 'We must go up and take possession of the land because we can certainly conquer it!' But the men who had gone up with him responded, 'We can't go up against the people because they are stronger than we are!' So they gave a negative report to the Israelites about the land they had scouted: 'The land we passed through to explore is one that devours its inhabitants, and all the people we saw in it are men of great size. We even saw the Nephilim there. (The offspring of Anak were descended from the Nephilim.) 'To ourselves, we seemed like grasshoppers, and we must have seemed the same to them."

"Then the whole community broke into loud cries, and the people wept that night ... If only we had died in the land of Egypt or if only we had died in this wilderness! Why is the Lord bringing us into this land to die by the sword? Our wives and little children will become plunder. Wouldn't it be better for us to go back to Egypt?"

This scripture shows us how the spirit of fear, doubt, and unbelief was transferred from the ten spies' negative report onto the tribe of

Israel.

Also, you should know the person who wants to pray for you. If you do not know them, you do not know where their walk with the Lord is. They could have some open doors that you do not want to be transferred to you with them laying their hands on your head and praying. "Lay hands suddenly on no man, neither be partaker of other men's sins: keep thyself pure." 1 Titus 5:22 (KJV)

If someone comes to me that I do not know, and wants to pray for me, I immediately cover myself with the blood of Jesus (under my breath) and reach out and take their hands.
But, I will not let them lay hands on my head.

Prayer to Break Witchcraft, the Occult, and Transference of Spirits

I renounce the strongholds of Divination, the Occult, Witchcraft, Transference of Spirits, Freemasonry and other such organizations and lodges.

I renounce all their manifestations and fruits including:

- Idolatry
- Sorcery
- Rebellion
- Disobedience
- Ouija board
- Fortune tellers, soothsayers, and psychics
- Self will
- Mind control
- Satanism
- Santeria

I now renounce my involvement in any of these witchcraft practices in Jesus' Name. I renounce any practices or words that were involved in these practices in Jesus' Name. I now break and set myself free from every stronghold of Witchcraft in my life right now in Jesus' Name!

I also renounce the laying on of hands by any Christian or any other person who calls themselves a Christian that allowed the transference of any and all ungodly spirits. I now break and set myself free from every ungodly spirit in Jesus' Name!

I also renounce any and all access rights that were opened by me or a family member of mine who participated in Freemasonry, sororities, lodges, or fraternities.

I now break and close all doors to every spirit that operated through those organizations. I break their power over me now in Jesus' Name! Amen.

Word Curses

Our Words are powerful. Proverbs 18:21 (KJV) tells us "Death and life are in the power of the tongue" and those who love life will choose the positive words and confessions in life.

Word curses are when we or others continually confess negative upon ourselves. When we hear these negative confessions over and over again, our mind thinks they are true. Some examples: "I always get the flu," "I will never have enough money to buy a new car," "I am always sick." As we go through life confessing these curses on us, our mind starts to believe them. Then, when we want to make a positive confession like "I am healed in Jesus' Name," our mind gets confused. Are we healed or not? These word confessions actually become part of our lives and part of our personality.

A good example of this is Elijah the prophet. He just had a great victory in defeating Jezebel's prophets in II King 9:22. Jezebel becomes angry at Elijah and curses him, promising to kill him.

Elijah becomes so obsessed with these thoughts that he imagined the curses were true. He runs to the cave and is depressed.

Satan uses these negative confessions by others (and yourself) to keep us in poverty, sickness, fear, torment, and even death.

It's interesting to note that Scripture tells us that our sins are forgiven – but what about our words? "But I say unto you, that every idle word that men shall speak, they shall give account thereof in the Day of Judgment." Matthew 12:36 (KJV)

In 1968, a rock and roll radio station picked up a radio signal. It was in Japanese. When they had it translated, the message was from World War II, from the Japanese Homeland to a Japanese war vessel at Pearl Harbor. Apparently, this signal (words) were floating around in space until it was picked up in 1968.

Watch what you are saying!

ꓫPrayer to Break Word Curses ꓦ

Father, word curses can come from others and by my own negative confessions. I know I have cursed others and myself with my words. I know others have cursed me with their negative words also.

I ask you to forgive me for cursing individuals with my negative words and ask you to forgive those individuals who have cursed me with their negative words.

Your Word states "Death and life are in the power of the tongue. And those who love it will eat its fruits." Proverbs 18:21 (NKJV). Today I choose life. I hereby renounce all false prophecies, and word curses spoke over me by myself or other individuals in Jesus' Name.

I confess: I am not sick, not poor but walk in divine health, am prospering, and I have the mind of Christ, and I can do all things through Christ who strengthens me.

In Jesus' Name. Amen!

Vietnam War Veterans

Many Vietnam War veterans are still angry over the war, can never settle down, and still have no peace over the outcome of the war and the way they were treated when they returned home. These traits many times are passed down to their children.

When American GIs landed in Vietnam, Buddhist monks would surround the airfields, praying curses over them. These curses were the result of being in a war zone, have caused terrible destruction on our Vietnam War veterans and their families.

I have seen both Vietnam War veterans and their families be set free from these traits after going through and breaking these curses.[5]

Note: Also see "Erasing the Memories" about PTSD.

---

[5] Information for this page came from "Deliverance Manual", by Bill Sudduth, Righteous Acts Ministries.

Prayer for Vietnam War Veterans and

Their Spouses and Children

Father, I forgive my country and its citizens for the way they treated me when I returned from Vietnam.

I rebuke all the Buddhist monks' prayers that spoke curses over my family and me as I entered Vietnam.

Therefore, I break all curses of never finding peace, of always being angry, and always having a wandering spirit.

I now claim peace, my anger is gone, and I can settle down in Jesus' Name.

I also break all soul ties and any curses or transference of spirits from any and all prostitutes, in Jesus' Name. Amen.

Addictions

Many times as Christians we only deal with the fruit hanging on the tree of the struggles we go through in life but never get to the roots of the tree – the real problem. That is why people who get prayed for and seem to get relief or healed don't stay free, and those problems return again and again.

We must bind the strong man first "Or else how can one enter into a strong man's house, and spoil his good, except he first binds the strong man? And then he will spoil his house." Matthew 12:29.

One area in which I think we have done injustice to our brothers and sisters is with addictions.

When someone comes to us with an addiction, we tend to cast out the addiction – drugs, alcohol, sex, money, food, etc.

The problem is that we only cast out the addiction and leave the strong man.

Fully-grown tree with its fruit represents the strongman of rebellion with all its fruits of addiction.

That is why addicts once delivered usually return to their addiction shortly after they are delivered.

The root, or open door, the strong man of the addiction, is rebellion. The addict is rebelling against God's Word, his parents, and the world's authority.

When you cut down the tree of rebellion, the fruit will wither and die. The addict will be set free from the oppression of his addictions.

Once the tree is cut down all its fruit will die. Once the strongman is cast out all oppression from the addictions will dry up and wither away.

This prayer to break the addiction is to break the demonic oppression over that addiction or addictions. All addictions are deep rooted and shamed based. Your drug of choice, whether drugs, alcohol, food, sex, etc., is what you are using to numb the pain of your trauma and shame.

Again, this prayer to Break the Power of Addictions will break the spiritual oppression from that addiction.

But most individuals with addiction must work through their trauma and shame that caused them to numb the pain in the first place.

I went to counseling for two years to work on my issues of anger, shame, low self-esteem, etc. from being sexually abused. After I worked through my trauma, I then started working on being set free from my sexual addiction.

Those who struggle with addictions may need further help. There are many good Christian addiction programs and counselors to whom you can make yourself available.

Prayer to Break the Power of Addictions

Father, because rebellion is the root of all addiction, I renounce anything I said in rebellion against you, my parents, and others in authority over me.

I command all spirits of guilt, shame and condemnation to come out of my conscience in the Name of Jesus. I command all spirits of pride, stubbornness, disobedience, rebellion, self-will, selfishness, and arrogance to come out of my will in the Name of Jesus.

I now command the Root of Rebellion along with (name the addiction) to leave in Jesus' Name. All taste, smell, and desire for my drug of choice are gone.

I now break the power of the Stronghold of Rebellion and command it to leave me in Jesus' Name! Amen.

Smoking

Some people can quit smoking while others have struggled for years to quit. Those individuals who struggle with quitting tobacco have formed a habit and have given Satan access rights to continue to keep them in bondage.

When Christopher Columbus came to America, he found Native Americans smoking pipes that were called "calumets." According to Native American legend, "these pipes possessed supernatural power and a charming effect." The Native American legend continues stating "Tobacco was a sacred plant and burning it brought favor in the eyes of their gods." By smoking it and using the Calumet, they said it guaranteed their protection. The smoking of the peace pipe was also an offering to the demons above and below.[6]

The Old Testament warns us against the burning of incense to other gods. (II Kings 22:17,

---

[6] http://freeinthelordministries.com/SMOKING.htm

23:5; II Chronicles 28:25, 34:24-25; Jeremiah 1:16, 7-9, 11:12, 19:4.

Some people can quit smoking with no problems others seems to battle forever. I believe those who can't quit smoking are caught in this web of the idolatry of burning incense to other gods every time they light up and smoke a cigarette.

Prayer to Break the Addiction of Smoking

Father, in Jesus' Name, I repent for the burning of incense to other gods and forming a spiritually rooted stronghold in my life. I ask you to forgive me of this sin.

I renounce and break the power of the "Calumet" along with its power and charming effects, its possessed supernatural power, and it's guaranteed protection it had on my life.

I serve no other God than Jesus. I ask you to take the power, the taste, the cravings, and the emotional and spiritual effects of the use of tobacco from me now in Jesus' Name.

I thank you for setting me free this day in Jesus' Name! Amen.

The Power of Music

God made music to be one of the most powerful forces of expression and inspiration. The vibrations or sounds of music effect our emotions and our mind paints pictures with it. Music can bless us or curse us.

The most powerful angel in heaven was Lucifer. "His voice could be heard above the other angels ... The great sound that came from his throat sounded like timbrels, drums, and tambourines, stringed instruments, pipes, and flutes."[7]

A good example of music affecting an evil spirit is found when an evil spirit was tormenting King Saul. He calls David to play on his harp, and the evil spirit departs King Saul.

"And Saul's servants said to him, 'Surely a distressing spirit from God is troubling you. Let our master now command your servants, who are

---

[7] Destined For Dominion by A. L. Gill, Powerhouse Publishing, Frawskin, CA., 1991, page 14.

before you, to seek out a man who is a skillful player on the harp. And it shall be that he will play it with his hand when the distressing spirit from God is upon you, and you shall be well.' So Saul said to his servants, 'Provide me now a man who can play well, and bring him to me.' Then one of the servants answered and said, 'Look, I have seen a son of Jesse the Bethlehemite, who is skillful in playing, a mighty man of valor, a man of war, prudent in speech, and a handsome person; and the Lord is with him.' Therefore Saul sent messengers to Jesse, and said, "Send me your son David who is with the sheep...' And so it was, whenever the spirit from God was upon Saul, that David would take his harp and play it with his hand. Then Saul would become refreshed and well, and the distressing spirit would depart from him." I Samuel 16:15-19 & 23 (NKJV).

But in our society, it seems like Satan has control of the music world and has our children mesmerized by it. Demonic messages, words, names of bands such as Incubus[8] are part of

---

[8] See Appendix B.

Satan's plans to invade our minds with his music. Ungodly music has caused individuals to live ungodly lives, and even to commit suicide.

Prayer to Break the Power of Ungodly Music

In the Name of Jesus and through the power of His blood, I renounce, break, and sever all soul ties with all ungodly music, the songs, the artists, and groups.

I break the spirit of its inspiration and the spirit of those who performed it. I break the ungodly vibrations that touched my emotions and the ungodly pictures that it painted in my mind.

I break and renounce all demonic spirits behind that music and influences of those demonic spirits.

I now ask You, God, to forgive me for listening to that type of music and, in some cases, making music, the artist or groups, my idols.

I now renounce, break and set myself free from all ungodly influences of evil music in Jesus'

Name! Amen.

Part III
What About Those
Memories?

Dealing with Memories

All of our negative memories stay in our mind and affect us and our body until we deal with those memories.

If these negative memories are not dealt with, they can come out in all kinds of sickness, long term illness, and bondages. Eventually, those negative memories can lead to trauma.

That is why scripture tells us that we are transformed by the renewing of our mind. "And do not be conformed to this world, but be transformed by the renewing of your mind ...." Romans 12:2 (NKJV)

Remember my story on pages 18 and 19 and how I had to transform my mind for seven months confessing God's Word on healing.

Inner Healing

(Written by Rev. Barbara Bybel)

There are times in our lives when counseling is not enough. Things happen to us that scar us and change the direction of our thought processes. Whether these things are real or not doesn't matter. If something happened to you as a child and you perceived it as so, it was real to you and your entire life, from that point on, was based on that perception. I can give you an example:

When I was about 13 years old, my parents got divorced. Because no one really explained what was going on, I took responsibility for it. My perception was, if I had just been a better child, my dad wouldn't have left us. In reality, I had NOTHING to do with my parents' divorce. This traumatic event shaped my view of marriage and what it was supposed to be. I believed that I needed to get married young enough so that WHEN I got divorced, I still had enough time for the "real" thing. This became a self-fulfilled prophecy, at least the first part is. I am currently divorced.

Counseling did not touch the depth the trauma of that event marked on my soul. Divorce came into my life where there had been a marriage and then my own divorce later in life solidified to me that that is how it is supposed to be. I counseled for two years with my pastor, but I just couldn't get free of the toll this had taken on my soul, until...

Someone had come to our church ministering in prophetic inner healing. At that point, I didn't realize I was holding on to any of this. While being ministered to through inner healing, I allowed Jesus into that situation, and then He set me totally free.

We know that we are made up of body, spirit, and soul. When we accept Christ, our spirit aligns with the Lord's, but our soul has some work to do. This is where things that happen to us as children, teenagers or even as adults, show up. The soul is where the mark is left. This is why you can become a Christian and be saved in every sense of the word yet still struggle with circumstances of the past.

I have had the privilege of being trained by various individuals, people I call "generals" in the area of inner healing. There are, of course, many ways to accomplish inner healing, but the most important thing is to listen very carefully to the Holy Spirit. Here is an example of inner healing based on my training (not by any means the only way to do inner healing, but what I have found is the most effective for me):

An inner healing person came to our church for a conference. I knew I had hurts, but I wasn't quite sure exactly what they all were. The facilitator told the members of the group to close their eyes, and the Holy Spirit was going to show each person something they were ready to deal with. I was sitting next to my friend, and she began to cry. I heard people all over the room crying, and I just sat there saying to the Lord, "Please don't forget me." All of a sudden, I saw Jesus, and He had His hand extended to me.

I gave Him my hand, and He took me to the corner of a room. The room had no ceiling, and we were sitting in the corner at the top of the wall, with feet dangling. I had no clue where we were. I asked Him what was going on and He said: "Watch." All of a sudden, I saw my dad, and I knew where we were. We were in a hotel room, he was sitting on the edge of the bed, his head in his hands, and he was crying. I said, "Lord, what is this?" He said, "This is the day your dad left your house. This is how much he loved you." My parents were divorced when I was 13 years old. Subconsciously I thought it was easy for him to leave us because I never saw him cry. My dad was a Vietnam War veteran, and he did not show emotions at all. When the Lord showed me he was crying; I began to sob. He did care! I did not even realize that I felt like he did not care.

Inner healing brings Jesus into situations, and Jesus heals them. My job as a counselor is to help guide people through the process. My client may be a little fearful as I start ministering. I assure them that they are ready for whatever the Holy Spirit wants to show them. He is the one leading, He is the one who got them to this point, and He is the one that will guide them through their healing.

Assuming someone has a prayer life when going through inner healing, the inner healer must be what I will call "prayed up." To hear the Holy Spirit clearly, one needs to stay plugged in. It is imperative that the participants allow the Holy Spirit to lead the sessions; prayer is the key to staying plugged in. There have been times when I had a plan on how to minister in one area, but when we got in that room, things took a major turn, and we ended up totally somewhere else. These moments are welcome! The Holy Spirit knows best what the person being healed needs and knows what he or she can handle. It is vital to keep His agenda and remember to be led by Him.

When we are saved, the Holy Spirit dwells in us, period. This analogy helped me to understand the gifting's that are provided to us:

We already have the Holy Spirit in us when we are saved. When we are **baptized in** the Holy Spirit with the evidence of speaking in tongues, we get a toolbox. The Holy Spirit becomes the toolbox. That tool box holds gifting's which include word of wisdom, word of knowledge, prophecy, tongues and interpretation, faith, gifts of healing, working of miracles, discerning of spirits, diverse (or different) kinds of tongues. 1 Corinthians Chapter 12 – Holy Bible. The Lord has given these tools to each person, and the tools will vary, using some more than others do. My toolbox for inner healing contains all the tools above, but I use prayer, visualization and the prophetic most often.

Inner healing is a very personal ministry, and while we should be eager to minister it and go through it, there are few cautions as well.

When ministering to someone, remember that your clients trust you with their very personal and private things and this should be a reminder of the privilege the Lord has given you. You should treat each person with the utmost compassion. This includes looking out for the best way to minister to that particular person and keeping their personal and private matters, just that ... personal and private. If someone is going through inner healing and is being sexually abused, physically hurt or going to hurt someone else or themselves, you must take it to the next level up the chain of command just as you would in counseling.

It is important to remember **NEVER to suggest an issue to anyone. An example of this would be "Are you sure you haven't been molested." If this person was molested, it is the Holy Spirit's job to show them. Remember, He knows when that person is ready to accept and what he is not yet ready for. One time when ministering to someone, I knew he had been molested, but he did not. I just kept working with him and, in time, the Holy Spirit revealed this. We dealt with the situation, and he is totally free today.

There are many sources for inner healing, and I would like to caution you to seek a denomination that has a solid foundation based on the Word of God. Ask questions. See what the source believes. Do not let just anyone minister to you. Others can minister differently than me, you, or anyone else but what they are saying and how they are leading you MUST line up with the Word of God.

Inner healing is not hard. As stated earlier, you can also do this at home, by yourself. I have done this many times. I sit in a quiet room and just pray. My prayer would be something like:

Holy Spirit, I submit myself to you. I pray right now that you roll the movie of what it is you would have me deal with today.

Then I just sit and wait. When He shows me something, I just ask Him questions. I have asked Him things such as: What is that? Why do I see that? What does it mean? What do you want me to do? After each encounter, it is VITALLY IMPORTANT that you discuss this with your spiritual leader. He or she is your covering and should be aware of what is happening with you spiritually. I always go to my senior pastor or another pastor on staff at my church and "bounce" things off them. I do not want to be hanging out on a limb all by myself; neither should you.

I leave you with this prayer:

Holy Spirit, I pray that you would prepare the hearts of the people reading this book to be totally set free. I pray that any fear would be gone in the Name of Jesus and that your perfect peace would rest upon them. I pray for heavenly direction as to how and where to obtain this ministry. I pray for guidance should they be doing this by themselves. I know you want the person reading this book to be totally set free because you have done this for me and you do not love me anymore than you love them. I thank you right now for blessing their steps in walking in complete healing. I am thanking you right now for the miraculous results and God; you get all the glory.

I pray this in Jesus' Mighty Name. Amen.

Trauma

If negative memories are not dealt with, they can turn into trauma.

Even though you may pray for healing, if the trauma is not dealt with, you may not be healed. A good example of this comes from Joan Hunter's Ministry. She states that a man had a car accident and needed much healing. He went to all the popular healing ministries, yet he was not healed. When he came to her service, Joan did not pray for healing but prayed a trauma prayer over him. Immediately he was healed.

The trauma that was still in this man's body from the accident was stopping his healing. If you have been prayed for many times and have not received your healing, then deal with the trauma – it might be stopping your healing.

This is why we pray for those who have had body part transplants. The trauma from that person dying stays with those body parts, and when transferred to you, you can experience some of the same sickness, bondages, and trauma that that person had experienced.

Blood transfusions and body parts contain someone else's blood. That is why we go through Generational Curses with you. The curse is in the blood.   If you have had any of the above mentioned, please break all ungodly soul ties and generational curses that may have come down through that individual's bloodline.

Some of you may think this is extreme.   I would rather err on the abundance of caution than leave something undone. Remember, "It's the little foxes that spoil the vines."

Erasing the Memories

But can we really be free of all those negative memories that we have accumulated over our lifetime? How do we get rid of the abuse, pornography, bad marriages, chronic illness, etc.?

When I first heard that God could take away the negative memories, I was skeptical. Read my story in my book "*The Un-Shattering of the Soul.*" You will read that after I was prayed for, the memories of the abuse and the pornography were gone! I knew I was abused, but I could not bring up any of the negative images, which used to cause negative emotions. My mind was totally set free![9]

Shortly after that, I prayed the trauma prayer for a Vietnam War veteran who had PTSD. His memories of the sights and sounds of the war are gone. He can now sleep restfully all night

---

[9] For a complete understanding please read Freedom *Beyond Comprehension* by Joan Hunter Ministries.

long. He was even discharged from his psychologist.

My mind is now clear without the images; sounds or smells of the abuse or pornography or sexual images. Satan no longer torments me with those things.

Yes, you too can totally be set free!

Praying the Trauma Prayer

(Erasing Your Negative Memories)

 Please take the time to go through this book to fully understand how Satan obtains access rights in us and makes strongholds in our soul.

 Once you have read the book, understand its principles, and go through all the prayers – then you are ready for this Trauma Prayer.

Trauma Prayer

Father, in Jesus Name, I forgive all individuals who have caused trauma in my life.

I know what they did to me will always be wrong, but I choose to release them to you.

I now release all negative memories, videos, pictures, smells and desires, the guilt, shame, pain, anger, and any other ungodly emotion that came in through the physical, sexually, verbal or spiritual trauma.

I choose this day to release the pain and ask you to wipe away all the negative, and all the bad memories from this trauma down to the cellular level of my brain, never to return, in Jesus' Name. Amen.

Keeping Your Deliverance

"When an unclean spirit comes out of a man, it roams through waterless places looking for rest, and not finding rest, it then says, 'I'll go back to my house where I came from.' And returning, it finds the house swept and put in order. Then it goes and brings seven other spirits more evil than itself, and they enter and settle down there. As a result, that man's last condition is worse than the first." Luke 11:24-26 (HCSB)

This Scripture tells us that once delivered; it is our responsibility to fill up the area(s) that were cleansed and delivered. How do we do this?

Praying, reading your Bible, listening to Christian music, attending church services more than once a week, and joining a small group for encouragement will help you "fill up your house," your spiritual man.

If you were set free from any addiction, you should see a Christian counselor who can help you work through your wounds. It is also a good idea to get an accountability person that you can trust and talk with about the trials you are going through, asking them to help keep you on track with your deliverance. This should be someone who can keep your confidentially of the personal things you talk together about.

Let me say another thing at this point: If you have gone through this book and are doing the things for "Keeping Your Deliverance," there may be times that you "fall" back into some area of sin again.

This does not mean you are not delivered. Your mind and actions need to catch up with your newfound freedom. Do not let Satan tell you that you are not delivered. Repent and tell Satan and yourself that you are free from that sin and move on. If you need more assurance, you can go through the deliverance prayer again.

Satan attacks us daily, so we need to continue to fill up our spiritual man daily. This will be a lifelong project of renewing our mind.

Appendix A

What If I Need More?

I have seen amazing results as individuals have closed the doors to all of Satan's access rights previously opened in their lives.

There are some, however, that no matter how hard they try and no matter what access rights or doors they close, it still seems they cannot get a victory in their life. That person may need deeper deliverance.

This type of deliverance would be one-on-one in counseling type sessions. *The Refuge House* has done hundreds of these types of deliverance. If you feel you need this type of deliverance, please call us for more information.

Scripture itself mentions 16 other spirits that would need to be dealt with.

Spirit of Antichrist.

1 John 4:3 (KJV) "And every spirit that does not confess that Jesus Christ has come in the flesh is

not of God: and this is that **spirit of antichrist**, whereof ye have heard that it should come; and even now already is it in the world."

Spirit of Bondage

Romans 8:15 (KJV) "For ye have not received the **spirit of bondage** again to fear, but ye have received the Spirit of adoption, whereby we cry, Abba, Father."

Deaf and Dumb Spirit

Mark 9:25 (KJV) "When Jesus saw that the people came running together, he rebuked the foul spirit, saying unto him, Thou **dumb and deaf spirit**, I charge thee, come out of him, and enter no more into him."

Last Enemy Death

1 Corinthians 15:26 (KJV) "The last **enemy** that will be destroyed is **death.**"

Spirit of Divination

Acts 16:16 (KJV) "And it came to pass, as we went to prayer, a certain damsel possessed with a **spirit of divination** met us, which brought her masters much gain by soothsaying."

Spirit of Error

1   John 4:6 (KJV) "We are of God; he that knoweth God heareth us; he that is not of God heareth not us.   Hereby know we the spirit of truth, and the **spirit of error**."

Familiar Spirits (notice plural)

Leviticus 19:31 (KJV) "Regard not them that have **familiar spirits**, neither seek after wizards, to be defiled by them: I am the Lord your God." Spirit of Fear

2   Timothy 1:7 (KJV) "For God hath not given us the **spirit of fear**, but of power, and of love, and of a sound mind."

Spirit of Haughtiness

Proverbs   16:18   (KJV)   "Pride   goeth   before destruction, and a **haughty spirit** before a fall." The Stronghold of Heaviness with a Root of

Rejection

Isaiah 61:3 (KJV) "To appoint unto them that mourn in Zion, to give unto them beauty for ashes, the oil of joy for mourning, the garment of praise for the **spirit of heaviness**; that they might be called trees of righteousness, the planting of the Lord, that he might be glorified."

Spirit of Infirmity

Luke 13:11 (KJV) "And, behold, there was a woman which had a **spirit of infirmity** eighteen years, and was bowed together, and could in no wise lift up herself."

Jealousy

Proverbs 6:34 (NKJV) "For **jealousy** is a husband's fury: therefore he will not spare in the day of vengeance."

Lying Spirit

2 Chronicles 18:22 (KJV) "Now, therefore, behold the Lord hath put a **lying spirit** in the mouth of these thy prophets, and the Lord hath spoken evil against thee."

Perverse Spirit

Isaiah 19:14 (KJV) "The Lord hath mingled a **perverse spirit** in the midst thereof: and they have caused Egypt to err in every work thereof, as a drunken man staggereth in his vomit."

Seducing Spirits (Notice plural)

1 Timothy 4:1 (KJV) "Now the Spirit speaketh expressly, that in the latter times some shall depart from the faith, giving heed to **seducing spirits**, and doctrines of devils."

Spirit of Whoredoms (notice plural)

Hosea 5:4 (KJV) "They will not frame their doings to turn unto their God: for the **spirit of whoredoms** is in the midst of them, and they have not known the Lord."

Appendix B

What about the Demonic

While I know that a Christian cannot be demon-possessed, I believe Christians can be hindered, harassed, influenced or tormented and can give Satan access rights to attack us.

If you were ever sexually abused or were or are currently struggling with sexual addiction, you will need to deal with the following sexual demons.

Incubus and Succubus

Two such sexual spirits are Incubus and Succubus. "The word Nightmare itself comes from the Anglo-Saxon neaht or nicth (= night) and Mara (= an agent, so that Mara from the verb Merman, literally means a "crusher," and the connotation of a crushing weight on the breast is common to the corresponding word in allied language."[10]

---

[10] David J. Hufford, *The Terror That Comes in the Night: An Experience – Centered Study of Supernatural Assault Traditions,*

The word "nightmare" was used in the 1300th century, and it referred to an evil female spirit afflicting sleepers with a feeling of suffocation. By the 1350s, the term used was "nytmare" and by 1440, it was "Nyghte mare" with the word Mare meaning goblin. In the 16th century, nightmare was used to describe, "a bad dream caused by an incubus" and by 1829, it has the meaning of today "a bad dream" in general.

According to one legend, the incubus and his female counterpart, the succubus, were fallen, angels. The belief in these demons has been particularly prevalent in the "Middle Age", and stories of assaults by incubi were not uncommon.

"The fifteenth-century Christian believed that "wet dreams" (nocturnal emissions) resulted from intercourse with tiny spiritual creatures called incubi and succubus, a notion put forth in

(University of Pennsylvania Press, Philadelphia, PA 1982), page 54.

a papal bull ... the person who had wet dreams was guilty of sodomy as well as witchcraft."[11]

There are similar spirits in many cultures. In current usage, incubus means "a person or thing that oppresses, such as a nightmare."[12]

"An incubus poses as the Lord or Angel of Light or as a benign and loving spirit in order to seduce women sexually."[13]

The incubus spirit attacks females and can bring the women to climax. The female version of this spirit is the succubus and can bring a man to ejaculation. Although society relates these two demons to mythology and legend, I have dealt with several female clients that were attacked by this incubus spirit. Both women said they could feel this spirit touching them and could feel the

---

[11] Janet Shibley Hyde and John D. DeLamater, *Understanding Human Sexuality*, (McGraw-Hall Press, 2000), page 4.

[12] The Columbia Encyclopedia, sixth edition (Columbia University Press, 2000), pages 23 and 83.

[13] John and Mark Sanford, *A Comprehensive Guide To deliverance and Inner Healing*, (Fleming H. revel, MKK 1992) page 247.

pressure as though someone was lying on top of them.

In a recent article, *Attack of the Incubus*, Jamie Licauco, states that there have been documented cases of Nuns being sexually molested by Incubus in the middle ages. "Also a case in Chartres, France where this spirit harassed a whole Convent."[14]

Unclean Spirit

"Spirits of uncleanness not only tempt parents and others to molest and commit incest, they enter the victim[15] through those activities."

The Bible tells us that both Jesus and Christians alike have authority over unclean spirits. Jesus cast a legion of unclean spirits out of a man into pigs, which caused the pigs to run over a cliff and kill themselves. Mark 5:13 (KJV).

---

[14] Sexual Molestations by Spirits – Attack of the Incubus, Inquirer News Service, October 8, 2001.
[15] Sanford, page 250.

Several times, we read about unclean spirits being rebuked by Jesus in Mark 9:25 (KJV) and Luke 9:42 KJV). We as Christians are given authority over these unclean spirits and, eventually, all unclean spirits will be cast into prison.

In Revelation 16:13 (KJV), we are told that the unclean spirits manifested themselves as frogs.

The Female Night Demon

Another spirit that must be dealt with is described in Isaiah 34: 1-17 (KJV). In these verses, Isaiah the prophet is describing the Judgments of the Nations. In verse 14, it states, "the screech owl also shall rest there…" The Hebrew word for "Screech Owl" in this verse is Lilith or a night Specter (an appearance or apparition). This word comes from the Hebrew root word layiah that means a twist (away from the light or figuratively an adversary). We also notice in this verse that the screech owl (Lilith) will "find for herself (female) a place of rest." Lilith then is an apparition at night of an adversary.

She is called the Female Night Demon. In mythology, Lilith is said to have been in the Garden of Eden and was Adam's first wife and that she is the mother of the two spirits Incubus and Succubus.

In later versions of the Bible, the word "screech owl" is translated as such:

> Night owl (Young 1898)
> Night Monster (ASV 1901, NAS 1995)
> Night Hag (RSV 1947)
> Night Creature (NIV 1978, NKJV 1982, NLT 1996)
> Nightjar (New World Translation 1984)
> Vampires (Moffatt Translation 1922)[16]

These demons are very real and powerful and can set up strongholds in our lives. These demons need to be dealt with to free ourselves from their effects or torments.

If you have gone through any of the experiences I have gone through, sexual abuse or sexual addiction, or are still struggling with

---

[16] Wikipedia, the free Encyclopedia – Lilith. http://en.wikipedia.org/wiki/Lilith

sexual addiction, I suggest you have someone with the knowledge of demons take you through deliverance from the specific sexual demons I mentioned above.

About the Author

Dr. (Rev) Paul E. Scull is founder and director of *The Refuge House.* He has been on staff at Chestnut Assembly of God for 30 years and has been in Counseling, Healing and Deliverance Ministry during that time. He has his doctorate in Christian Counseling and Psychology from the Carolina University of Theology and is an ordained minister. Dr. Scull has been married to his wife Rev. Eileen Scull for 45 years. They have two children, Michael and Amie, and one grandson, Keith.

He has written several books.

- *The Shattering of the Soul*
- *The Un-Shattering of the Soul*
- *The Animals* Tell His Story
- *Assembly of God Missionaries Caught Behind Enemy Lines During World War II* (due out 2017)

All books can be purchased from Amazon and other online bookstores. *The Un-Shattering of the Soul* is also available on Kindle.

You can also write Dr. Scull at *The Refuge*

House, 2554 E. Chestnut Avenue, Vineland, NJ 08361. For more information, call 856-691-1205. Dr. Scull is also available for speaking engagements.